Prayer

The First Step in Reaching

Your Community

Participant's Guide

Dwight Marable

TCN
TRANSFORMING
CHURCHES
NETWORK

Table of Contents

Introduction

Americans are people of action. We see a need, begin assessing the steps involved to meet that need and engage. In fact, we are so achievement oriented that we are up to our eyeballs in constant, ceaseless activities. Sleep deprivation is one serious health issue. Surveys indicate that the only people who work more intensely are the folks who live in Hong Kong.

Not only are we hard working, but thanks to Steve Jobs and friends, we are always connected to those we care about, communicating 24/7 with each other on issues that are important to us. The younger generations are addicted to constant communication. Even when in the same household or sitting across the table in a restaurant, they often prefer texting over face-to-face conversation.

In the midst of a world that is so globally connected, somehow we have lost contact with our Father. Action has replaced meditation. We have lost the art of conversation with the One who deeply loves us. David's repose, "I have stilled and quieted my soul; like a weaned child with its mother, like a weaned child is my soul within me" (Ps. 131:2). His further instruction to "Be still, and know that I am God" (Ps. 46:10) is one we rarely follow.

Prayer, the art of sharing our deepest thoughts, hopes and aspirations with God, while listening to the small, quiet response within is one most of us rarely experience. Yet, as we seek to engage those who do not know Christ, we need to engage Him first. It is His passion that drives us. We need to connect with His deep love that wants "no person to be lost." Somehow, in the mystery of partnership with Christ in fulfilling His mission, He wants us to ask, seek and knock, that the doors of our community might be opened to us as we carry out his commission of reaching the world with the Gospel.

Connecting with Our Father

Objective: *Why is it so tough to connect with the One who loves us so much? In this session, we will discover common prayer hindrances and how to move beyond them.*

Discovery Activity

Play Dough Creations

Learning Activity

Praying with a Purpose

Our Father in heaven. "Here God encourages us to believe that He is truly our Father and we are His children. We therefore are to pray to Him with complete confidence just as children speak to their loving Father."
  (from *The Small Catechism*, Dr. Martin Luther, part three, p. 8)

One of the most challenging aspects of the Christian life is found in prayer. Survey the average church-goer around the nation and you will discover that most people agree that prayer is important but spend very little time praying during any given week. Why is that? Why is prayer so difficult for so many? Why do so many people feel guilty about the time that they are spending in prayer? For most, there is at least one reason which can be identified as a block. Consider the six "prayer blocks" below and see if you can find your own experience in any one of them.

Prayer Blocks

Block #1: Prayer is boring.
A number of Christians are bored to tears with prayer. When we are bored with anything in life, we generally tend to avoid it. Prayer for many is dry as chalk dust or can be likened to eating a slice of toast with nothing on it. It all seems like a trivial ritual that has very little meaning or sense of satisfaction attached to it.

Block #2: My mind wanders.
Ever start to pray about something only to find your mind hopelessly wandering in a million different directions? Many are frustrated by

prayer because they find that it is incredibly difficult to get their minds to stay focused.

Block #3: I feel awkward.
A large number of Christians have never prayed aloud before. The idea of hearing themselves talk out loud to God generates feelings of awkwardness. Most of us don't like to feel stupid or inadequate, so for many it's safer to stay silent rather than stepping out of our comfort zone.

Block #4: Prayer doesn't make a difference.
Most of us would never admit to saying something this outrageous. But many Christians behave like prayer doesn't make a difference. Why bother engaging in an activity that is meaningless and pointless?

Block #5: I don't have the time.
In our rush-rush culture many are living time-poor lifestyles. Prayer sounds nice, but frankly, where would I find the time to pray? I'm racing from sun up to sun down and I have no margin in my life. Many have become too busy to pray.

Block #6: I don't know how to pray.
Reciting a creed or The Lord's Prayer are meaningful and authentic expressions of faith for many. However, for many Christians, praying to God in their own words is a real challenge. What do I say, what words do I use, and what should I pray about are common concerns for people that don't know how to pray.

So how about you? Which prayer block or blocks do you wrestle with? There could be one major stumbling block or there could be a combination of sticking points for you. You are not alone. Your frustration and disillusionment with prayer is shared by many. However, this series on prayer is an invitation for you to "become more than you are" when it comes to praying. It's an invitation to overcome whatever is hindering you from experiencing greater satisfaction in prayer. God wants times of prayer to be rich for His children and He wants to teach you how to pray.

Discussion Questions:
1. Which of the prayer blocks has been your experience?

2. What kinds of words would you use to describe your experience of prayer?

Praying the Lord's Prayer

Through the ages, Christians have returned again and again to the Lord's Prayer which Jesus outlined in Matthew 6:9-13:

> Our Father in heaven,
> hallowed be your name,
> your kingdom come,
> your will be done
> on earth as it is in heaven.
> Give us today our daily bread.
> Forgive us our debts,
> as we also have forgiven our debtors.
> And lead us not into temptation,
> but deliver us from the evil one.

A shortened version of the Lord's Prayer is also found in Luke 11:2-4. However, in Luke 11:1, a very important interaction takes place that needs to be highlighted right up front. A nameless disciple was watching Jesus for some time. We don't know exactly how long he observed Jesus' life, but we do know that He was impressed by His prayer life. And he asked Jesus a very profound question when he said, "Lord, would you teach us to pray?" There is something commendable in his question. It demonstrates an eagerness and a profound sense of openness. He is a man who wants to grow, and he wants to know how to pray more meaningfully. Something about the way that Jesus prays has caught his attention. Who better to learn from regarding prayer than the Lord Himself? As you start the Prayer Series, will you join hands with this man by allowing the Lord to teach you more about prayer? All you need as we get started is a willingness and an openness to learn. The Lord will meet you the rest of the way.

"Our Father in Heaven"

Jesus instructs us to start off our prayer by addressing God as "Our Father." Consider the following story from one man's life:

A few years ago, I was huddled with a group of men in a mountain cabin for a planning and goal-setting retreat. At the beginning of the meeting, the leader asked each of the nine men gathered to share about what we had been learning about being dads. It was a most unusual question for a group of men to talk about with one another. However, as each man took his turn to discuss what he had been learning about being a father, tears welled up in their eyes. All nine men began to cry when they talked about their kids. Some were going through very challenging seasons of parenting while others were enjoying times of pure delight. But one thing was apparent to all of us...these men loved their children. The depth of emotion that was displayed was quite extraordinary, and it left a deep imprint upon my mind and heart. For a few brief moments, I had a glimpse of how God must feel about His children.

When we start off a time of prayer, this is the kind of picture God wants us to have of Him. Jesus consistently called out to God as Abba, or Father, which is a term of great emotion and intimacy. Abba is not found as an Old Testament term for God but is a New Testament understanding of our fresh and open relationship with God.

Prayer is then about connecting with our heavenly Dad. It's a way for us to relate, to be open, and to be close. He wants us to approach Him, to be honest with Him, to share with Him, to open up to Him, and to be authentic with Him. He wants us to appreciate and to understand how high and deep and wide His love is for us. He is a Father who cries when He thinks about you.

Discussion Question:

• What principles from the article are you most challenged by and why?

Application Activity

A Letter to Dad

Instructions: Take 10-15 minutes on your own to a write a letter to God with the perspective that He is your Dad. This is a letter to Dad. What's on your mind these days? What kinds of things are you worried about?

What are you excited about or thankful for? In what ways are you disappointed or discouraged? How do you feel about your relationship with Him lately? Is it close or distant? Tell Him about how you feel. Simply use this as a time to talk to God honestly about what's going in your world.

Discussion Questions:

1. What was the writing experience like for you?

2. Would anyone be willing to share what they have written with the group?

Hallowed Be Your Name

Objective: *What does a potter do? In this session, we will seek to better understand the character of God and how we are called to honor Him with our praise.*

Discovery Activity

Play Dough Creations

Learning Activity

"Hallowed be Your Name"

In the previous session, we explored the implications of addressing God as our Father. The Lord, He wants us to experience all of the fullness of what it means for Him to be our Father. He desires closeness and authenticity with each of His children. Through the ages, Christians have returned again and again to the Lord's Prayer which Jesus outlined in Matthew 6:9-13:

> Our Father in heaven,
> hallowed be your name,
> your kingdom come,
> your will be done
> on earth as it is in heaven.
> Give us today our daily bread.
> Forgive us our debts,
> as we also have forgiven our debtors.
> And lead us not into temptation,
> but deliver us from the evil one.

One of the Biblical word pictures that describes our relationship with God in a different manner is taken from the world of pottery. God is pictured as the potter, and we are depicted as the clay – His work of art. As we consider the Lord's Prayer in greater detail, multiple images taken from the realm of the potter's wheel will be used to stimulate our thinking about prayer.

The phrase "Hallowed be Your Name" is not the kind of wording that we are accustomed to hearing in today's world. When Jesus used the word "hallowed," what He was communicating is that God's name certainly is holy in itself and we ask in this prayer that we may keep it holy.

"God's name is hallowed whenever His word is taught in its truth and purity and we as children of God live in harmony with it."
(from *The Small Catechism*, Dr. Martin Luther, part three, p. 8)

As we consider the image of God as the master potter, we are encouraged to ponder His reputation. He is to be exalted and appreciated for His works of art. He creates outstanding pieces of sculpture! There is none like Him in all the world…never before in history nor in ages to come.

When we address God in this way, it helps us keep proper perspective. When we pause to linger over the reality that God's name is hallowed, it reminds us that He is the potter and we are the clay. So often we get that mixed up in our minds. In fact, the culture we live in celebrates the notion that we are in control of our destiny. We can and should shape our futures. Our lives are what we make of them. However, if we are not careful, we get caught up in the lie of our day that suggests that we are both the potter and the clay. This is a subtle yet vicious distortion of the grand Heavenly scheme that the Lord has constructed. When we take the time to pray "hallowed be your name," we are admitting that God truly is the one in control and that He is the one that shapes our lives. He is the one who knows the number of hairs on our head. He is the one who numbers our days.

With this in mind, here are a few suggestions for expanding and lingering on this section of the prayer.

• Think about friends who need the love of God in their lives. You can pray that God will become more and more real to them this week. Ask God to reveal Himself as the Master Potter to those for whom you are praying. Pray that the Holy Spirit would make it evident to them that there truly is a God in Heaven who is shaping their lives.

• Use the Psalms as a way to praise God. Pick a psalm each day as a way to recalibrate your heart and your mind about who God really is.

• Pick different letters of the alphabet and spend time thanking God by thinking of words that begin with each certain letter. For example, for the letter "M" you could thank God that He is mighty, majestic, and merciful. For the letter "F" you could appreciate that God is faithful, forgiving, and our Father. Be creative and allow God to bring words to mind that you can pray back to Him.

- Play a few songs from a music CD that has words that focus on God's character and reputation. Music has a wonderful way of helping our hearts and minds focus on the majesty of our Lord.

Discussion Questions:
1. What kinds of things do you most appreciate about God?

2. What principles from the article are you most challenged by and why?

Application Activity

Prayer Blitz

Homework

This week make it your goal to have at least three different prayer times by using the "Letter to Dad" framework and adding a section where you are focusing on an idea from "hallowed be Your name." If you are comfortable simply talking out loud to God about your concerns and praise then simply "talk to Dad." Remember, the only way we learn to pray is to pray. It is like anything in life.

Your Kingdom Come

Objective: *How do we bring the Kingdom to our community? In this session, we will discover what it means to touch the world around us with the ways of the Kingdom of God.*

Discovery Activity

A Walk through the Community

Discussion Questions:

1. What were your thoughts and feelings as you walked in the community?

2. What needs, hurts, and issues might be present in this community?

Learning Activity

"Your Kingdom Come, Your Will Be Done"

In the previous modules, we have explored the implications of addressing God as our Father and praising Him by focusing on the phrase "Hallowed be your name." The Lord wants us to experience all of the fullness of what it means for Him to be our Father. He desires closeness and authenticity with each of His children. Through the ages, Christians have returned again and again to the Lord's Prayer which Jesus outlined in Matthew 6:9-13:

> Our Father in heaven,
> hallowed be your name,
> <u>your kingdom come,</u>
> <u>your will be done</u>
> on earth as it is in heaven.
> Give us today our daily bread.
> Forgive us our debts,
> as we also have forgiven our debtors.
> And lead us not into temptation,
> but deliver us from the evil one.

In the last section, the image of the potter's wheel was introduced. When we pray "hallowed be Your name," we are reminding ourselves that God is the master potter and we are the clay He is shaping. Let's consider the potter's wheel for a moment. Before an individual can work with a piece of clay it must be carefully and painstakingly placed in the center of the potter's wheel. If the clay is off-center, the potter will have an extremely difficult time shaping a cup, jar, or dish.

And so it is with our lives, our churches, and our communities. Life is best lived in the center of the potter's wheel. The center of the wheel represents God's best – His will for our lives. Blessed is the man or woman who strives to live in the center of God's will. When we pray that God's kingdom would come and His will would be done we are acknowledging our desire to live a life that is pleasing to Him.

"God's Kingdom comes when our heavenly Father gives us His Holy Spirit so that by His grace we believe His holy word and live a godly life now and in heaven forever."
(from *The Small Catechism*, Dr. Martin Luther, part three, p. 9)

PrayerWalking

In hundreds of cities across the globe, ordinary believers are prayer-walking through the streets of their communities. They pray while walking, with eyes open for the spiritual awakening God is bringing. In other words, Christians are taking their prayers into the communities in which they live. This has become a practical method for praying for God's kingdom to come and for His will to be done. For many this might be a new or novel idea, praying while walking, but rest assured it can be an enjoyable and uplifting experience. Here's what one Christian has to say about prayerwalking:

One evening my wife and I were strolling through our neighborhood. As we passed different homes we simply asked God to make Himself known in each of the homes we passed. We were asking God to draw our neighbors to Himself. When we got to one home, I had a strange idea pop into my head. You see, I knew that this neighbor was in the midst of bitter lawsuit regarding thousands of dollars. Our neighbor had been clearly wronged by a contractor and the next day there was going to be a major show-down in a courtroom. So, with a little apprehension, we walked up to his house and knocked on the door. After exchanging brief pleasantries, I simply blurted out, "Tony, I know that tomorrow is a big day for you in court and I was wondering if we could pray for you just a minute." He was visibly moved that we would care enough to even suggest the idea. I didn't pray long but I did ask God for justice and for a clear sense that our neighbor would be able to recover his money.

Later in the week, Tony stopped by on his own initiative to report the happy news…the judge had ruled in his favor! The point I wish to make is a simple one…the thought to pray for my neighbor happened while I was passing his home on a prayerwalk. There was something about being out in the street that created the opening in my mind and heart.

There is no set pattern or proven formula for prayerwalking. Prayerwalkers have set out with every imaginable style. There is nothing magical about praying while walking. God's Spirit is helping us to pray in the midst of the very settings in which we expect Him to answer our prayers. We instinctively draw near to those for whom we pray. Getting close to the community focuses our prayer. We sharpen our prayers by concentrating on specific homes and families. We enlarge our praying as well, crying out for entire communities to know God's healing presence.

Prayerwalks give us a simple way to fill the streets with prayer. Many are praying city-size prayers while ranging throughout their towns with disciplined regularity in small bands of two or three. Quiet triumphs often follow as God changes the city, day by day, and house by house.

Creative things to Pray during a Prayerwalk:

1. Attempt to keep every prayer pertinent to the specific community you pass through. As you do, you will find prayers naturally progress to the nation and to the world.

2. Use a theme passage of Scripture. Unless God guides you to use another, try 1 Timothy 2:1-8. Many have found it to be a useful launching point for prayerwalking. Verse 8 speaks of the important dimension to prayer connected with God's desire that all people be saved. "I want the men in every place to pray." Copy this and other passages in a format easy to read aloud several times during your walk. Each of the following prayer points emerges from this passage.

3. Concerning Christ: Proclaim Him afresh to be the one Mediator and the ransom for all. Name Him Lord of the neighborhood and of the lives you see.

4. Concerning Leaders: Pray for people responsible in any position of authority – for teachers, police, administrators, and parents.

5. Concerning Peace: Cry out for the godliness and holiness of God's people to increase into substantial peace. Pray for new churches to be established.

6. Concerning Truth: Declare openly the bedrock reality that there is one God. Celebrate the faithful revelation of His truth to all peoples through ordinary people (1 Tim. 2:8). Pray that the eyes of minds would cease to be blinded by Satan so that they could come to knowledge of the truth.

7. Concerning the Blessing of God: Thanksgivings are to be made on behalf of all people. Give God the explicit thanks He deserves for the goodness He constantly bestows on the homes you pass by. Ask to see the city with His eyes, that you might sense what is good and pleasing in His sight as well as what things grieve Him deeply. Ask God to bring forth an enduring spiritual awakening.

8. Concerning the Church: Ask for healing in relationships, that there be no wrath or dissension among God's people. Ask that God would make His people, men and women alike, expressive in worship with the substance of radiant, relational holiness. Ask that our worship would be adorned with the confirming power of saints doing good works in our communities.

Discussion Questions:
1. What stood out to you as you read about prayerwalking?

2. What principles about prayerwalking challenge you the most? Why?

3. What questions or reservations do you have about praying while you walk in your community?

Discussion Activity

Prayer Instructions—1 Timothy 2:1-8

¹I urge, then, first of all, that petitions, prayers, intercession and thanksgiving be made for all people—²for kings and all those in authority, that we may live peaceful and quiet lives in all godliness and holiness. ³This is good, and pleases God our Savior, ⁴who wants all people to be saved and to come to a knowledge of the truth. ⁵For there is one God and one mediator between God and mankind, the man Christ Jesus, ⁶who gave himself as a ransom for all people. This has now been witnessed to at the proper time. ⁷And for this purpose I was appointed a herald and an apostle—I am telling the truth, I am not lying—and a true and faithful teacher of the Gentiles. ⁸Therefore I want the men everywhere to pray, lifting up holy hands without anger or disputing (1 Timothy 2:1-8).

Discussion Questions:

1. Why do you think Paul uses the phrase "I urge" in 2:1?

2. What are some of the differences between requests, prayers, intercession, and thanksgiving?

3. What is the connection Paul is making between praying for "those in authority" and the kind of lives we experience in our communities?

4. How does verse 4 relate to what Paul has already talked about in 2:1-3?

5. What does Paul seem to be concerned about in 2:8?

6. What kinds of topics or requests does this passage indicate we are urged to pray about when it comes to others and our community?

Homework

This week make it your goal to take at least one prayerwalk in your neighborhood or community with an accountability partner. The prayerwalk can be a time of silently praying or a time to pray out loud – it is your choice. Use the information in the article on prayerwalking as your guide for ideas to incorporate into your prayerwalk.

Daily Bread

Objective: *What does it mean to rest in God? In this session, we will discuss how we can trust God with our lives to a greater degree.*

Discovery Activity

Name that Need

A few examples....
- Adam was alone so God gave him Eve.
- God met Sarah's need for a son by giving her Isaac.
- The Red Sea provided a way of escape for Israel.

Learning Activity

"Give Us Today Our Daily Bread"

In the previous modules, we have explored the implications of addressing God as our Father and praising Him by focusing on the phrase "hallowed be your name." The Lord wants us to experience all of the fullness of what it means for Him to be our Father. He desires closeness and authenticity with each of His children. The third module injected the idea of prayer- walking as a creative way to pray that God's kingdom and will be established in our lives and communities. In this section, we will explore the portion of the Lord's Prayer that centers on the phrase "our daily bread" from Matthew 6:9-13:

> Our Father in heaven,
> hallowed be your name,
> your kingdom come,
> your will be done
> on earth as it is in heaven.
> Give us today our daily bread.
> Forgive us our debts,
> as we also have forgiven our debtors.
> And lead us not into temptation,
> but deliver us from the evil one.

For a few weeks we have been talking about clay and the potter's wheel image. Clay needs two things to become something useful – pressure and water. The skilled hands of the potter carve and mold clay into the intended image that the artist has in mind. And yet, throughout the shaping process on the potter's wheel, generous amounts of water are applied to the clay to keep it malleable.

So it is with our lives. We have needs and our heavenly Father is keenly aware of them. Yet, we are encouraged by Jesus in the Lord's Prayer to make our requests known to God. And so, it is fitting, that we ask God to meet our most pressing daily needs. Daily bread can take on a broader meaning as we consider going to God with a variety of needs. When we move to this part of the prayer, it is important that we remember Jesus is encouraging us to ask God to meet our needs, not simply our wants. God is not to be pictured as our heavenly buddy, or the great vending machine in the sky. But rather, He is a loving Father who encourages us to ask.

"God gives us daily bread, even without our prayer, to all people, though sinful, but we ask in this prayer that He will help us to realize this and receive our daily bread with thanks. Daily bread includes everything needed for this life, such as food and clothing, home and property, work and income, a devoted family, an orderly community, good government, favorable weather, peace and health, a good name, and true friends and neighbors."
(from *The Small Catechism*, Dr. Martin Luther, part three, p. 10)

A posture of asking keeps us humble and dependent. It is a sure-fire way to help us remember that we are the clay; we are the ones that need the hands of the potter to lovingly shape us and apply water to our souls to keep us malleable. What then are we to ask for? Consider these "daily bread" areas of your life:

Friends who need God: Remember your friends who need a relationship with God. As you pray for them by name on a regular basis pray that the truths of the Lord's Prayer would become real to them. Pray that they will discover that they have a Heavenly Father to whom they can take their needs.

Wisdom: We need wisdom as we navigate through our day. There may be a major decision that you are faced with or a spur of the moment circumstance that comes out of nowhere.

Courage: It takes boldness to reach out in a broken world. Some times it is not convenient or you may be apprehensive. Join hands with the Apostle Paul who asked others to pray that he would have the courage to be a witness for Christ in his spheres of influence. A part of your daily bread might be your need for courage with your friends and contacts that need God.

Love: No greater love has a man than to lay down his life for his friends. Today, your need might be for a greater demonstration of love toward another. Or perhaps you do not feel very loved right now. Tell your heavenly Father exactly how you feel and ask Him to meet your longing.

Strength: Sickness and injury is a part of the human experience. Stress and the pressures of life can take a toll on any one of us. There are times when we need a fresh sense of God's resurrection power pulsating through our veins.

Resources: Is it a bill? A debt? A job? Where are you feeling the pressure financially right now? Go to God with that need and ask Him to provide you with what you need to make it through "this day."

Relationships: God wants us to go to Him with the significant issues that have surfaced in your key relationships. Is there a broken or fractured relationship that needs mending? Are you hiding anger or bitterness over something in your relational world? Take those needs to the Lord in prayer.

Discussion Questions:
1. What stood out to you as you read the article?

2. What principles from the article are you most challenged by and why?

3. What questions or reservations do you have about praying for daily bread in this way?

Application Activity 1

Instructions: Your assignment is to write out a "Daily Bread" prayer to God. Use the categories that were mentioned in the article to frame your writing. You are simply asking God to provide "daily bread" for yourself and others by using those categories. Use this as a time to be real and honest with God.

Application Activity 2

Father, I want to ask for wisdom about…

Father, I want to ask that you would bring complete healing for…

Father, I ask that you give me courage to…

Father, in this relationship, help me to…

Homework

This week, make it your goal to have two prayer times that focus on "daily bread" requests. If you are more comfortable writing your prayers, then use the "Daily Bread" prayer exercise as your template for your time with God. Also, feel free to incorporate other aspects of the Lord's Prayer that you have learned about in this series.

Forgive Us
Our Debts

Objective: *Can we walk in forgiveness? In this session, we will find guidance about living as a clean vessel who can hold pure water.*

Discovery Activity

Discussion Questions:
1. What were some of the lessons you learned from your mistake?

2. What are some ways that God uses mistakes to grow us?

Learning Activity

"Forgive Us Our Debts"

In the previous modules, we have explored a number of fresh and creative ways to pray through the Lord's Prayer. It's not meant to be a trite, formulaic kind of prayer. Rather, it is a model or template that we can use to have extended times of prayer before our heavenly Father. God wants us to experience all of the fullness of what it means for Him to be our Father. He desires closeness and authenticity with each of His children. Secondly, we focused on unique ways that we can declare "hallowed be Your name" as we consider the character and reputation of God. The third module injected the idea of prayerwalking as a creative way to pray that God's kingdom and will be established in our lives and communities. And, from the last meeting and for homework, you were encouraged to go to God with "Daily Bread" needs in your life.

"We ask in this prayer that our Father in heaven would not hold our sins against us and because of them refuse to hear our prayer. And we pray that He would give us everything by grace, for we sin every day and deserve nothing but punishment. So we on our part will heartily forgive and gladly do good to those who sin against us."
(from *The Small Catechism*, Dr. Martin Luther., part three, p.10)

In this section, we will explore the portion of the Lord's Prayer that centers on the phrase "forgive us our debts" from Matthew 6:9-13:

> Our Father in heaven,
> hallowed be your name,
> your kingdom come,

> your will be done
> on earth as it is in heaven.
> Give us today our daily bread.
> <u>Forgive us our debts,</u>
> <u>as we also have forgiven our debtors.</u>
> And lead us not into temptation,
> but deliver us from the evil one.

In his book, *A Layman Looks at the Lord's Prayer,* Phillip Keller recounts a personal story involving a potter in the back streets of Pakistan. Keller had asked the elderly man if he could watch him work his craft on a potter's wheel. With his consent, Keller followed the Pakistani man into a dank, dark room away from the bustling shops. The potter had begun to spin the potter's wheel when:

> Suddenly, as I watched, to my utter astonishment, I saw the stone stop. Why? I looked closely. The potter removed a small particle of grit from the goblet. His fingers had felt its resistance to his touch. He started the stone again. Quickly he smoothed the surface of the goblet. Then just as suddenly the stone stopped again. He removed another hard object - another tiny grain of sand – that left a scar in the side of the clay.
>
> A look of anxiety and concern began to creep over the aged craftsman's face. His eyes began to hold a questioning look. Would the clay carry within it other particles of sand or grit or gravel that would resist his hands and wreck his work? Would all his finest intentions, highest hopes, and wonderful wishes come to nothing?
>
> Why is my Father's will – His intention to turn out truly beautiful people – brought to naught again and again? Because of their resistance, because of their hardness. Why, despite His best efforts and endless patience with human beings, do they end up a disaster? Simply because they resist His will, they will not cooperate, they will not comply with His commands. His hands – those tender, gentle, gracious hands – are thwarted by our stubborn wills.
> (from *The Inspirational Writings of Phillip Keller,* p. 205-206)

Sin in our lives is a lot like grit. Sin in many ways represents resistance in our lives to the work of the master potter. He is shaping and molding our lives on the potter's wheel. Yet we often cling to attitudes, habits, thoughts, and behaviors that act as "gritty" opposition to the Master's hands. Jesus is making it very clear: we must confess the grit in our lives. We must come clean before the Lord and ask Him to cleanse us from all unrighteousness. When we do that on a regular basis, 1 John 1:8-9 reminds us that God is faithful and just to forgive us of our sins.

Let's be honest though; it takes courage and humility to come to God with sin in our lives. It can be much more comfortable to stay in denial. But that is just what the enemy of our souls wants. Satan knows that unconfessed sin, which stays in the darkness, has a way of interfering with God's work in our lives. This part of the Lord's prayer is a reminder that we must be diligent to not let grit remain hidden. Name your sins specifically, as the Holy Spirit brings them to mind and receive the cleansing that your soul, mind, and heart need.

One final thought…forgiveness of personal sin has a direct connection with the command to forgive others. When Jesus taught the Lord's Prayer, He made it clear – we are to forgive others just as we ourselves have received forgiveness. Often, this is easier said than done and requires a choice of our wills. Granting forgiveness to others is never easy, especially when someone else has thrown "grit" on to our lives. I often want to say, "Would you please keep your grit to yourself, I have enough in my own life without you helping me out…thank you very much!" With this in mind, keep short accounts of wrongs that others have inflicted upon you. Believe it or not, it is in your own best interest to let the debt go, rather than harboring bitterness and resentment. Choosing to forgive will grant freedom and vitality in your life. That is why Jesus connected the two ideas together when He taught on forgiveness of sin.

Discussion Questions:
1. What stood out to you as you read the article?

2. What principles from the article are you most challenged by and why?

3. What questions or reservations do you have about asking God for forgiveness?

4. What challenges do you face in forgiving others?

Application Activity 1

Instructions: Take some time on your own to allow God to remind you of unconfessed sin in your life. Allow the categories below to get you thinking about your thoughts and actions over the past 14 days. In your private time, simply ask God to bring to mind by His Spirit any area of your life that needs to be confessed and forgiven. Take a portion of time with each word and ask, "Father, is there any way that I have demonstrated _____ in the last 14 days?" If something comes to mind ask Him to forgive you and then move on to the next word. Feel free to do the whole exercise silently in prayer or if you are more comfortable use the space provided below to write out your prayers. You might want to use a phrase like, "Father, I confess that I have been _____ when I _____. I ask that you would forgive me and cleanse me.

Anger
Pride
Self-sufficiency
Not trusting God
Lust
Envy
Boasting
Self-pity
Resentment
Jealousy
Hurting another with my words
Negative attitude
Gluttony
Money or possession focused
Disobeying God
Lies or half-truths

Application Activity 2

Hopefully, by now the group is becoming a little more comfortable with the idea of praying aloud. This is another opportunity for people to pray with others about their needs. Ask people to pray briefly so that several can enter into the time of prayer. Ask the group to focus on the kinds of things they wrote down which they are comfortable praying about in front of others. If the group is comfortable you might want to split the group in half so each person can actually pray aloud more frequently. Ask people to use the pieces of the Lord's Prayer we have studied so far as an outline of the prayer time:

Part 1: Thank God that He is your Father and wants a close relationship with each of you.

Part 2: Spend time honoring and praising God for who He is.

Part 3: Ask God to establish His will in your life and in others (pray for specific examples that come to mind).

Part 4: Bring specific needs (yours and others) before God.

Homework

As we learned, forgiving others is a part of the Lord's Prayer. For homework, take some time to consider the notion of forgiving others. Often, without realizing it, offenses from others can build up in our heart. Grit has a way of building up if we are not careful. Take some time this week to ask God to reveal to you the people and the offenses that you have not forgiven. Make a list on paper as the Lord helps you remember. Forgiving others does not mean we simply "forget." Rather, it is a choice. We are choosing to forgive so that we can experience full freedom in Christ. Do not expect this to be easy. But it is well worth the effort!

For each person on your list, say aloud: "Father, I forgive _____ for (specifically identify all offenses and painful memories)_____".

Deliver Us From Evil

Objective: *How do we fight evil effectively? In this final session, we will discover how we stand against the devil and walk in victory.*

Discovery Activity

Take 10 minutes to write your own personalized Screwtape Letter. The assignment is to write a letter to a demon who is assigned to thwart, minimize, and deceive you. What would that strategy look and sound like? In other words, what would the strategy be for preventing you from living effectively for God? You won't be asked to share your letter with anyone so feel free to be authentic and honest in your writing.

Screwtape Letters (personalized)

Dear Wormwood,

Discussion Questions:
1. What was it like to write your own Screwtape Letter?

2. In your experience, how do most people perceive Satan and demons?

Learning Activity

Deliver Us From Evil

In the previous modules, we have explored a number of different ways to pray through the Lord's Prayer. It's not meant to be a trite, formulaic kind of prayer. Rather, it is a model or template that we can use to have extended times of prayer before our heavenly Father. God wants us to experience all of the fullness of what it means for Him to be our Father. He desires closeness and authenticity with each of His children. Secondly, we focused on unique ways that we can declare "hallowed be Your name" as we consider the character and reputation of God. The third module injected the idea of prayerwalking as a creative way to pray that God's kingdom and will be established in our lives and communities. The section on "Daily Bread" helped us to see that God is interested in meeting our daily needs and that He wants us to bring those petitions before Him. The fifth module challenged us to carefully consider our critical need for forgiveness of sin. God wants us to deal with "grit" in our lives and to also extend forgiveness to those that have sinned against us.

"We ask in this inclusive prayer that our heavenly Father would save us from every evil to body and soul, and at our last hour would mercifully take us from the troubles of this world to himself in heaven."
(from *The Small Catechism*, Dr. Martin Luther, part three, p. 11)

In this section, we will explore the portion of the Lord's Prayer that centers on the phrase "deliver us from the evil one" from Matthew 6:9-13:

> Our Father in heaven,
> hallowed be your name,
> your kingdom come,
> your will be done
> on earth as it is in heaven.
> Give us today our daily bread.
> Forgive us our debts,
> as we also have forgiven our debtors.
> <u>And lead us not into temptation,</u>
> <u>but deliver us from the evil one.</u>

Throughout this series, prayer is likened to the dynamic experience of an artisan working a piece of clay on a potter's wheel. Once the raw material has been shaped by the potter, it is set aside for a time before it is placed in a kiln to be cured. In Jeremiah 17:7-8, we find these words:

> But blessed is the man who trusts in the Lord, whose confidence is in Him. He will be like a tree planted by the water that sends out its roots by the stream. It does not fear when heat comes; its leaves are always green. It has no worries in a year of drought and never fails to bear fruit.

Heat and drought are a part of the human experience. We live in a broken world which is in active rebellion against our Lord. One of the consequences of the Fall is that pain and difficulty intersect all of our lives. It is not a question of "will the heat and drought come?" as it is "when will the heat and drought come?" How will you respond to the trial, the pressure, the temptation, or the flaming arrow from the enemy? All pieces of clay eventually find their way into the kiln…it is a part of the process of becoming a useful instrument for the will and pleasure of the potter.

Some works of clay do not respond favorably to the heat of the kiln. The blast from the furnace overwhelms some pieces of pottery and they crack under the oppressive pressure. Other cups, jars, and dishes are able to successfully withstand the experience and emerge as a useful instrument. When we get to this portion of the Lord's Prayer we are simply asking the Lord to help us not to crack. It is as if we are saying, "I know that the heat is coming…I know that the pressures of life are coming my way…help me to respond well and to hold up under the blast of heat."

Being placed in the kiln then is your lot in life. Your Father in heaven wants to give you the supernatural help and strength to endure the fiery ordeal. He wants to help you see the way of escape (1 Corinthians 10:13) and to choose to take that route. Sometimes we see the kiln coming and we can ask the Lord for His protective strength to be a "heat shield." Still other life experiences simply creep into our lives with the forcefulness of a tornado that has gone undetected. We desperately need His strength to not crack when life throws us a curveball The Lord's Prayer is a reminder that God wants us to bring all of our "kiln" experiences to Him. Asking for His help is a way to admit our weakness and our frailty.

Many believers are intimidated to discuss the reality of Satan. C.S. Lewis claimed that most Christians either give Satan too much credit and attention or completely ignore his existence. Peter reminds us in 1 Peter 5:8-9 that:

> Your enemy, the devil, prowls around like a roaring lion looking for someone to devour. Resist him, standing firm in the faith, because you know that your brothers throughout the world are undergoing the same kind of sufferings.

Some of the trials and difficulties that come our way in life are attacks of the enemy. And we are given the biblical command to resist him by standing firm in our faith. James 4:7 instructs us to "Submit yourselves, then to God. Resist the devil, and he will flee from you." The Lord's Prayer is a fantastic reminder about where the strength and courage must come from to resist the evil one. The power to resist and to stand firm must come from God and it is ours to grab a hold of if we will only pray. We need to regularly and consistently ask the Lord to deliver us from evil. We can ask God to be a hedge of protection, a fortress for our defense, a rock in the midst of the storm, our defender in the battle, and our shield from flaming missiles.

Discussion Questions:
1. What stood out to you as you read the article?

2. What principles from the article are you most challenged by and why?

3. What questions or reservations do you have about praying for protection from Satan and from temptation?

Discussion Activity

Read the following passage and discuss the questions:

> [10]Finally, be strong in the Lord and in his mighty power. [11]Put on the full armor of God, so that you can take your stand against the devil's schemes. [12]For our struggle is not against flesh and blood, but against the rulers, against the authorities, against the powers of this dark world and against the spiritual forces of evil in the heavenly realms. [13]Therefore put on the full armor of God, so

that when the day of evil comes, ycu may be able to stand your ground, and after you have done everything, to stand. [14]Stand firm then, with the belt of truth buckled around your waist, with the breastplate of righteousness in place, [15]and with your feet fitted with the readiness that comes from the gospel of peace. [16]In addition to all this, take up the shield of faith, with which you can extinguish all the flaming arrows of the evil one. [17]Take the helmet of salvation and the sword of the Spirit, which is the word of God. [18]And pray in the Spirit on all occasions with all kinds of prayers and requests. With this in mind, be alert and always keep on praying for all the Lord's people (Ephesians 6:10-18).

1. What does Paul want us to understand in verse 12?

2. Why does Paul want us to put on the whole armor of God (vs. 11)?

3. Why do you think Paul uses the word "stand" so often in this passage?

4. What might be some examples of a flaming arrow of the evil one (vs.16)?

5. How do you interpret the six pieces of armor mentioned in this passage?

6. What role does prayer play in "standing firm?"

7. What are you personally most challenged by in this passage?

Application Activity

Part 1: Thank God that He is your Father and wants a close relationship with each of you.

Part 2: Spend time honoring and praising God for who He is.

Part 3: Ask God to establish His will in your life and in others (pray for specific examples that come to mind).

Part 4: Bring specific needs (yours and others) before God.

Part 5: Ask for forgiveness of any sin in your life and choose to forgive others.

Part 6: Ask for God's strength in any trials you or others are facing and ask for protection from the work of the enemy.

Closing Activity

Discussion Questions:
1. What have been two personal highlights for you in going through this series?

2. What do you hope will be different in your life as a result of this series?

Close the meeting with a time of thanksgiving for all that God has done in the group.